Sand

By Margaret Clyne and Rachel Griffiths

Contents

What Is Sand?

Sand is many tiny pieces of rock.

How Is Sand Made?

Wind blows on rocks.
Rain falls on rocks.
Waves crash on rocks.

The wind, rain and waves
break the rocks into tiny pieces.
The rocks become sand.

Where Is Sand Found?

There is sand in deserts.

There is sand on beaches.

There is sand on dunes.

What Is Made With Sand?

sandcastle

hourglass

bricks

concrete